Burger Joints
BBQ SHACKS
SANDWICH SHOPS
Where America Eats

Publications International, Ltd.

Front cover: Meathead Goldwyn/AmazingRibs.com (top right); The Italian Store (bottom left); Mathew Lankford (top left); Jim Livermore (center); Shutterstock (top); Smoque (bottom right)

Back cover: Kasey Doshier (top left); Katz's Delicatessen (top right); © Soo Photography (bottom)

Tracy Aiguier, 41; David Allen, 182; Willie Allen, 127 (top & bottom); Tom Andrews, 16 (top, left & right), 17 (top, left & right); Maia Assaf, 78 (left, right & bottom), 79; Darrell Auld, 62 (top & bottom), 63; Tom Beck, 104 (top left, top right, bottom left & bottom right), 105; Becks Prime, 4, 5; Morgan Bellinger, 60, 61 (left & right); Big Jud's, 6 (left & right), 7 (top & bottom); Steven Biver, 150; Borinquen Restaurant, 132, 133 (top left, top right, center & bottom); P. Boutros, 142, 143; The Brick Pit, 74, 75; Justin Fox Burks, 76, 77; Tim Campbell, 130, 131; Capriotti's Sandwich Shop, Inc., 136 (top & bottom), 137 (top & bottom); Felicia Chen, 155 (top); Jeannie Choe, 144; Brad Cleveland, 70 (top & bottom), 71; Emanuel Cole, 183; The Counter, 15; Logan Cramer, 20, 21; Devil Doll, 134; Donna DeVor, 58, 59 (top & center); Diasphoto.com, 40 (left & right); Kasey Doshier, 29; Stephen Dugan, 141; Annette Dunning, 86 (top & bottom), 87; Jefferies Eldridge, 46, 47; Erick Riedell Photography, 10, 11, 66 (top & bottom), 67 (top & bottom); Charles P. Everitt, 140; Glenn Fieber, 52 (top left, top right, bottom left & bottom right), 53 (top & bottom); Rebecca Fondren, 88, 89; The Gallery Studios, 148, 149; Germantown Commissary, 84 (top, left & right), 85; Meathead Goldwyn/AmazingRibs.com, 106 (top, left & right), 107; Amy Gondeiro, 18, 19 (top & bottom); Tammy Green, 28 (bottom right); Art Guimond, 28 (top left, top right & bottom left); Mark Herron, 110; Huey's, 26, 27 (top, center & bottom); Jack Stack Barbecue, 82 (left, right & bottom), 83; Jonathan Jackson, 101 (top left & bottom left); Jimmy & Drew's Deli, 152 (top & bottom), 153; Joss, 56, 57 (top left, top right, bottom left & bottom right); Henrick Kam, 145; Katz's Delicatessen, 154; KennethHess.com, 138 (top & bottom), 139 (top); Ben Kessler/ unbreaded.com, 12; Ari Kleit, 13 (top & bottom); Scott Kuo, 155 (bottom); La Sandwicherie, 158 (top right & bottom), 159 (top); Mathew Lankford, 31, 49 (bottom); Debbie Lee, 36 (left & right); Seth M. Lee, 164, 165; Nigel Leeming, 34, 35; © Scott Levoyer, 96 (top & bottom), 97; Jim Livermore, 166 (top & bottom), 167; Chynna Lockett, 54 (top & bottom), 55 (top & bottom); Alex M., 112 (top & bottom), 113; Michael Majewski, 178, 179; Frank Marchese, 172, 173 (top & bottom); Steve Martin, Swami Studios, 72, 73; Melt Bar & Grilled, 162, 163; Memphis Minnie's BBQ Joint, 91; Jeremy Merriam, 8 (top & bottom), 9, 128, 129; Laura Miller, 92, 93; Miner-Dunn Hamburgers, 32, 33 (left & right); William Nancarrow, 180, 181; Michael Ngim, 14 (bottom); Karen Nicoletti, 123 (top); David Park, 37; Patrick Onofre Photography, 151; Dick Patrick, 111 (top & bottom); Rudy Peev, 14 (bottom center); Leah Pellegrini, 169; Phil's BBQ Point Loma, 94, 95; Poag Mahone's, 38, 39 (top left, top right, bottom left & bottom right); David L. Reamer, 168; Roper's Ribs, 98, 99 (top, center & bottom); Shutterstock, 99; Rosebud Steakhouse, 42; Rouge, 44, 45; Michael Rubenstein, 48, 49 (top); Sal, Kris, & Charlie's Deli, 174, 175; The Salt Lick, 100, 101 (top right & bottom right); Jack Scheffer, 22, 23; Jeff Schnorr, 184, 185; Scrise.com, 156 (top & bottom), 157; Elina Shatkin, 135 (right); Chris Shelton, 159 (bottom); Corey Shields, 160, 161; Mike J. Shin, 158 (top left); Jason Silvis, 30 (top, left & right); Cathy Slyman, 80 (top & bottom), 81; Snow's BBQ, 108, 109; © Soo Photography, 102, 103; Stan's Bar-B-Q, 114 (top & bottom), 115; Dustin Steller, 24 (left & right), 25; Steve Adams Studio, 68, 69; Ryan Stiner, 188; Aaron Stout, 122, 123 (bottom); Super Smokers BBQ, 116, 117; Susan Chen Huddy Photography, 135 (left); Anthony Tahlier, 43 (top); TJ Lambert Stages Photography, 50 (left & right), 51; Tuyen My Nguyen, 186, 187; Ubon's Barbeque of Yazoo, 118, 119; Uncle Bub's BBQ & Catering, 120, 121 (top & bottom); David VanHook, 176, 177; Mike Vasiliauskas, 170, 171; Vincent A Restaurant, 64 (top & bottom), 65; Virgil's Real BBQ, 124 (top & bottom), 125; Valissa Warren, 59 (bottom); Dan Watkins, 146, 147; Michael Wu, 43 (bottom); Benny Yeh, 14 (top & top center); Crystal Zawatski, 139 (bottom)

ISBN-13: 978-1-4508-1769-1
ISBN-10: 1-4508-1769-6

Library of Congress Control Number: 2010940577

Manufactured in China.

8 7 6 5 4 3 2 1

Publications International, Ltd.

Table of Contents

BECKS PRIME Restaurants®

HOUSTON, TX
Multiple Locations
www.becksprime.com

WHAT'S IN IT?

> Two slices of thick cheese (American, Swiss, Cheddar or Danish Blue)

> Thick slices of crispy bacon

> Homemade hickory or Becks Prime Sauce

> Ripe red tomatoes

> Fresh lettuce

> Homemade guacamole

> Sautéed onions

ALWAYS FIRST QUALITY WITH 10% BUTTERFAT GUARANTEED
BECKS PRIME
EXTRA STOUT
MILKSHAKES
HOUSTON, TEXAS

What's in it?

- 3 ounces mayo
- 3 ounces ketchup
- $1/4$ ounce mustard
- 12 to 15 dill pickle slices
- $1\frac{1}{2}$ cups shredded lettuce
- 4 slices tomato

- 4 slices Cheddar cheese
- Thick-sliced bacon
- Sautéed mushrooms
- Sautéed onions
- Fresh-baked 8-inch bun

1289 Protest Rd., Bosie, ID 83706
(208) 343-4439
www.bigjudsboise.com

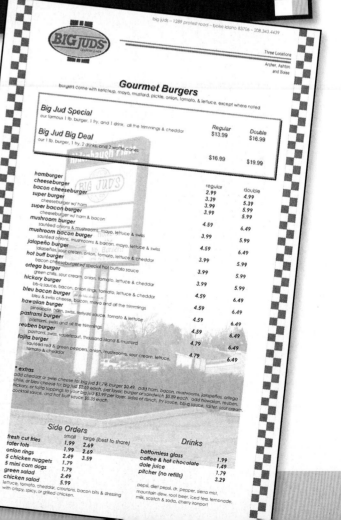

big juds – 1289 protest road – boise idaho 83706 – 208.343.4439

BIG JUDS

Three Locations

Archer, Ashton and Boise

Gourmet Burgers

burgers come with ketchup, mayo, mustard, pickle, onion, tomato, & lettuce, except where noted

Big Jud Special	Regular	Double
our famous 1 lb. burger, 1 fry, and 1 drink, all the trimmings & cheddar	$13.99	$16.99
Big Jud Big Deal		
our 1 lb. burger, 1 fry, 2 drinks and 2 waffle cones		
	$16.99	$19.99

	regular	double
hamburger		
cheeseburger	2.99	4.99
bacon cheeseburger	3.39	5.39
super burger	3.99	5.99
cheeseburger w/ ham		
super bacon burger	3.99	5.99
cheeseburger w/ ham & bacon		
mushroom burger	4.59	6.49
sautéed onions & mushrooms, mayo, lettuce & swiss		
mushroom bacon burger	3.99	5.99
sautéed onions, mushrooms & bacon, mayo, lettuce & swiss		
jalapeño burger	4.59	6.49
jalapeños, sour cream, onion, tomato, lettuce & cheddar		
hot buff burger	3.99	5.99
bacon cheeseburger w/ special hot buffalo sauce		
ortega burger	3.99	5.99
green chile, sour cream, onion, tomato, lettuce & cheddar		
hickory burger	3.99	5.99
bb-q sauce, bacon, onion rings, tomato, lettuce & cheddar		
bleu bacon burger	4.59	6.49
bleu & swiss cheese, bacon, mayo and all the trimmings		
hawaiian burger	4.59	6.49
pineapple, ham, swiss, teriyaki sauce, tomato & lettuce		
pastrami burger	4.59	6.49
pastrami, swiss and all the trimmings		
reuben burger	4.59	6.49
pastrami, swiss, sauerkraut, thousand island & mustard		
fajita burger	4.79	6.49
sautéed red & green peppers, onion, mushrooms, sour cream, lettuce, tomato & cheddar	4.79	6.49

* **extras**

add cheddar or swiss cheese to: big jud $1.79, burger $0.49, add ham, bacon, mushrooms, jalapeños, ortega chile, or bleu cheese to: big jud $2.69 each, per layer; burger or sandwich $0.89 each. add hawaiian, reuben, hickory, or fajita topping to your big jud $3.99 per layer, sides of ranch, fry sauce, bb-q sauce, tarter, sour cream, cocktail sauce, and hot buff sauce $0.35 each.

Side Orders	small	large (best to share)		Drinks	
fresh cut fries	1.99	2.69		bottomless glass	
tater tots	1.99	2.69		coffee & hot chocolate	1.99
onion rings	2.49	3.59		dole juice	1.49
5 chicken nuggets	1.79			pitcher (no refills)	1.79
5 mini corn dogs	1.79				3.29
green salad	2.49				
chicken salad	5.99				
lettuce, tomato, cheddar, croutons, bacon bits & dressing with crispy, spicy, or grilled chicken.				pepsi, diet pepsi, dr. pepper, sierra mist, mountain dew, root beer, iced tea, lemonade, milk, scotch & soda, cherry ironport	

Can you conquer the famous one pound BIG JUD?

BLACK IRON BURGER SHOP

540 E. 5TH ST. • NEW YORK, NY 10009
(212) 677-6067 • www.blackironburger.com

What's in it?

HORSERADISH CHEDDAR

2 (4-OUNCE) PATTIES

GRILLED RED ONIONS

TOMATO

BURGER STATION
There Is A Difference Too

Here at the Burger Station we serve an old-fashioned hamburger. We grind and patty our meat daily. We cook each burger to the customers' specifications. Our normal "everything" includes fried onions, mustard and pickle.

What's in it?

- *fried onions*
- *mustard*
- *pickle*
- *cheese*

113 E. 7th Ave., Winfield, KS 67156
(620) 221-9773

BUTCHER SINGER

1500 WALNUT ST. • PHILADELPHIA, PA 19102
(215) 732-4444 • WWW.BUTCHERANDSINGER.COM

WHAT'S IN IT?

10 OUNCES DRY-AGED PRIME BEEF

FRIED ONIONS

ENGLISH CHEDDAR

CREAMY RUSSIAN DRESSING

THE COUNTER®
CUSTOM BUILT BURGERS

Multiple Locations, www.thecounterburger.com

Veggie burger

The Counter's veggie burger is hand-formed and made with brown rice, spinach, panko bread crumbs, mushrooms, onions, corn, black beans, zucchini, red bell peppers and carrots. The veggie burger and veggie toppings are completely vegan and cooked separately from meat products.

Toppings

Imported or domestic aged cheeses
• Danish Blue Cheese • Greek Feta • Gruyère • Herb Goat Cheese • Horseradish Cheddar • Imported Swiss • Sharp Provolone • Tillamook Cheddar

Locally sourced toppings
• Bermuda Red Onion • Black Olives • Dill Pickle Chips • Dried Cranberries • Grilled Pneapple • Hard Boiled Eggs • Jalapeños • Roasted Chiles • Roasted Corn & Black Bean Salsa • Scallions • Spicy Pepperoncinis • Sprouts

Scratch sauces
• Apricot Sauce • Caramelized Onion Marmalade • Country Buttermilk Ranch • Ginger Soy Glaze • Honey Mustard • Peanut Sauce • Red Relish • Roasted Garlic Aioli • Russian Dressing• Spicy Sour Cream • Sweet BBQ Sauce

Bun
• English Muffin • Hamburger Bun • Honey Wheat Bun • "Burger in a Bowl" with a lettuce blend or mixed baby greens

What's in it?

- sharp provolone cheese
- lettuce blend
- tomato
- fried onion strings
- sautéed mushrooms
- sun-dried tomato vinaigrette

108 N. 7th St.
Salina, KS 67401
(785) 825-2699
www.cozyburger.com

What's in it?

ketchup
mustard
grilled onions
dill pickle

The Cutting Board

307 Dewey Ave., Eureka, MT 59917 • (406) 297-6090
www.thecuttingboard.biz

The Eureka Bubba Burger is a mesquite-grilled burger with spicy sausage, jumbo shrimp and a smoky chipotle sauce.

What's in it?

chipotle sauce

green leaf lettuce

roma tomato

red onion

pickle

Cheddar cheese

Cajun sausage

jumbo shrimp

What's in it?

~15-pound burger ~onions

~pickles ~mayonnaise

~lettuce ~cheese

~tomatoes

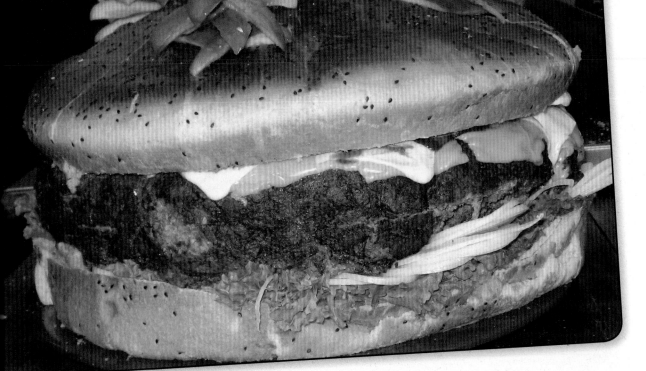

Nationally known as the home of the "World's Largest Hamburger Challenges"—this is where it all began!

Denny's Beer Barrel Pub

1452 Woodland Rd., Clearfield, PA 16830
814-765-7190 • www.dennysbeerbarrelpub.com

HEMMER BROTHERS
Burgers & Fries

230 S. Phillips Ave. #101 • Sioux Falls, SD 57104
(605) 334-3301

The unique thing about our bacon cheeseburgers is that we grind the bacon in with the ground beef. We do that for a few different reasons. First, you get bacon flavor in every bite. Second, your bacon is never burnt or too fatty. And, third, it lets our customers know that we really do grind our burgers fresh every day. In fact, it's usually only an hour or two since the burger has come out of the grinder and we're grilling it for our customers. We only put beef in our burgers, no fillers whatsoever. The only time we add anything other than beef is if we're doing a bratwurst burger or something like that. We grill our burgers on a flat top grill so that they get a nice crust on the outside. Then we melt on either American, Cheddar, pepper jack or provolone cheese and put them on an old-fashioned toasted bun. We let our customers finish them at our toppings bar. We try to keep things pretty simple. It's kind of that "why mess with a good thing" mentality. We do some feature burgers occasionally to keep things new for our customers. Those can include a bratwurst burger, mushroom Swiss, grilled onion garlic melt, the champ, BBQ-cheese-hamburger, the fireball, cream cheese burger or the Italian stallion.

WHAT'S IN IT?

2 freshly ground beef patties	pickles
bacon	onions
cheese	tomatoes
	lettuce

What's in it?

1/4 pound lean meat	pickle
American cheese	onion
lettuce	Hi Boy Sauce
tomato	5-inch bun

Our burger is set apart from others, first by only using fresh, quality 90% lean meat along with the freshest produce. Our burgers are smashed down on a hot grill which sears in the juices and preserves the flavor.

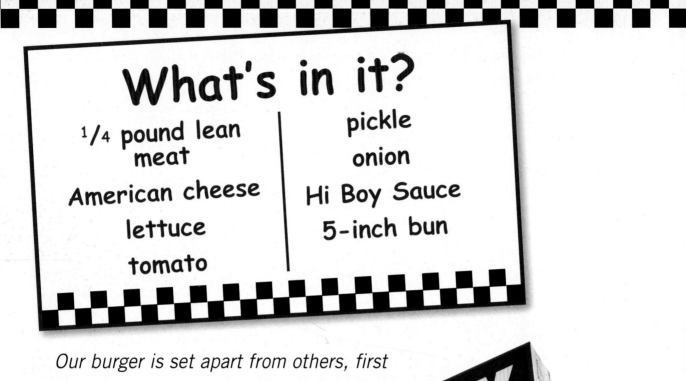

HI BOY

DRIVE-THRU

Multiple Locations • www.hiboydrivein.com

HUEY'S ®

Multiple Locations • www.hueyburger.com

WHAT'S IN IT?

mayo	onion
mustard	cheddar or Swiss cheese
lettuce	toasted sesame seed bun
tomato	
pickles	

Huey's burgers are 80/20 chuck ground fresh daily, topped with World Famous Seasoning (a secret recipe) and cooked to order on a flat grill, making certain not to flatten or squash the burger down while cooking to preserve the juiciness.

BEST BURGERS
IN CHICAGO!

2900 W. Belmont Ave., Chicago, IL 60618
(773) 604-8769 • www.kumascorner.com

KUMA'S
Corner

WHAT'S IN IT?

Avocado	Lettuce
Cherry peppers	Tomato
Pepper jack	Red onion
Chipotle mayo	Pretzel roll

TAKE OUT

LUNCHBOX LABORATORY

THE ART AND SCIENCE OF AMERICAN COMFORT FOOD

Lunch, Dinner, Brunch & More

WWW.LUNCHBOXLABORATORY.COM

7302 15th Ave. NW., Seattle, WA 98117
www.lunchboxlaboratory.com
206-706-3092

LUNCHBOX
Laboratory

What's in it?

Monterey Jack cheese

7 pieces maple bacon

Jalapeños

Sautéed onions

Mama Lil's Goathorn Pepper Sauce

Kaiser roll

8940 Indianapolis Boulevard, Highland, IN 46322
(219) 923-3311

What's in it?

- 87% lean choice beef
- Old English Cheddar
- relish
- tomatoes
- lettuce
- mustard

Our meat is uniquely lean—we're the only one you'll find that uses 87% lean choice beef—and it's that which provides our hallmark taste: juicy without being greasy. To achieve this savory, old-time flavor, we hand-form each patty, add a special blend of seasonings, and cook it on a flat grill.

Murphy's

11 S. Main St. | Hanover, NH 03755 | (603) 643-4075
www.murphysonthegreen.com

What's in it?

8 ounces Angus beef
American cheese
crispy fried shallots
remoulade

lettuce
tomatoes
bacon
ciabatta roll

Pearl's
DELUXE BURGERS

708 Post St., San Francisco, CA 94109
(415) 409-6120 • www.pearlsburgers.com

Pearl's Bula Burger was voted
one of the five best burgers in
San Francisco by *San Francisco
Weekly* (May 28, 2008).

Bula BURGER

What's in it?

Thick-cut bacon
Homemade onion rings
Jack cheese
Bula Sauce
Artisan French roll

What's in it?

9-ounce sirloin beef patty

2 slices American cheese

3 strips bacon

lettuce

tomato

egg bun

Poag Mahone's was included in Alan Richman's July 2005 *GQ Magazine* article:

"20 Hamburgers You Must Eat Before You Die"

8 High St., Boston, MA 02110 • (617) 426-1234
www.radiusrestaurant.com

What's in it?

- 80% lean ground beef
- horseradish sauce
- good-quality Vermont or English Cheddar cheese (thick slices)
- crispy onions
- brioche bun

The real trick here is the olive oil and not cooking the
burger directly on the grill the entire time. This is a messy,
coma-inducing burger so make sure you don't have to operate
any heavy machinery any time soon after eating it, and be sure
you have a cozy spot for a quick nap. Try this burger once and
you will never want to serve it another way.

www.rosebudrestaurants.com

ROSEBUD

restaurants

WHAT'S IN IT?

- 🌹 12 OUNCES 80% LEAN PRIME GROUND BEEF
- 🌹 LETTUCE
- 🌹 TOMATO
- 🌹 PICKLES
- 🌹 CHEESE
- 🌹 ONIONS
- 🌹 PRETZEL ROLL BUN

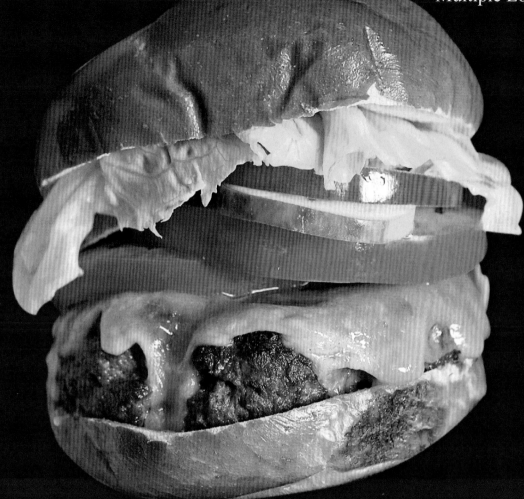

"The burger is a massive 12 ounces, and so juicy the kitchen should consider issuing bibs. The burger, cooked precisely to order, arrives on a soft but chewy pretzel-dough bun that handles the juicy meat without falling apart, and the flavor—with or without melted cheese—is sensational."

- Phil Vettel, *Chicago Tribune* restaurant critic, June 2005

What's in it?

12 ounces fresh
ground beef

Gruyère Cheese

Caramelized
onions

Lettuce

Tomato

Challah
roll

ROUGE

205 S. 18TH ST., PHILADELPHIA, PA 19103

(215) 732-6622 • WWW.ROUGE98.COM

Slap Daddy's

914 Baytree Rd., Valdosta, GA 31602 • (229) 244-1966
www.slapdaddys.com

What's in our burgers?

ketchup	sautéd mushrooms	A1® Sauce
salsa	green chilis	guacamole
mustard	jalapeños	fried egg
mayo	pickles	chili
tomato	relish	slaw
lettuce	banana peppers	bacon
sliced onions		Texas Toast or grilled bun
grilled onions	BBQ sauce	

Slow Bar

533 SE. Grand Ave. • Portland, OR 97214 • (503) 230-7767 • www.slowbar.net

What's in it?

Gruyère cheese

Butter lettuce

Tomato pickle relish

House-made beer-battered onion rings

Toasted brioche bun

Milwaukee, WI
1900 W. St. Paul Ave.
414-931-1919

What's in it?

beef patty
Cheddar cheese
Swiss cheese
American cheese
bacon
fried onions
diced jalapeños
country butter roll

Sobelmans
PUB —N— GRILL

www.milwaukeesbestburgers.com

What's in it? →

- 2 (1/3-pound) sirloin patties
- Solly's special mayo
- raw Spanish onion
- Solly's special stewed onions
- grilled mushrooms
- Wisconsin butter
- 1 slice Wisconsin American cheese
- 1 slice Wisconsin Swiss cheese
- lettuce
- tomato

Butter Burgers • Sandwiches • Fish Fries • Pies • Malts

SOLLY'S Grille

The Original Butter Burger
Breakfast • Lunch • Dinner

414-332-8808

Open Seven Days a Week
Est. 1936

4629 N. Port Washington Rd., Glendale, WI 53212

The "Bubba" Burger is unlike any other burger out there. It is grilled to perfection on our well-seasoned grill and topped with only the best ingredients available. This burger is irresistible!

What's in it?

grilled onions	KC Masterpiece® BBQ Sauce
bacon	pepper jack cheese
jalapeños	grilled buttered Kaiser bun

SUGAR SHACK

22495 Hwy. 385, Deadwood, SD 57732
(605) 341-6772

What's in it?

- ◆ Super Sauce
- ◆ lettuce
- ◆ tomato
- ◆ onion
- ◆ pickles
- ◆ grilled pineapple
- ◆ teriyaki sauce

Multiple Locations • www.teddysbiggerburgers.com

Columbus, OH

Thurman Cafe

What's in it?

- bun
- mayo
- lettuce
- tomato
- pickle
- hot pepper
- 12-ounce burger

- bacon
- Cheddar cheese
- another 12-ounce burger
- sautéed onion
- mushrooms

- ham
- American cheese
- provolone cheese
- top bun

183 Thurman Ave. • Columbus, OH 43206 • (614) 443-1570
www.thethurmancafe.com

25°

TWENTYFIVEDEGREES

proudly serving since 2004

Multiple Locations
www.25degreesrestaurant.com

What's in it?

lettuce
tomato
pickle
sweet onion
jack cheese

organic beef
bacon
brioche roll
avocado or jalapeños (optional)

Burger Joints **61**

What's in it?

Pickled red onion

Grace's Mustard

Whidbey slaw

Whidbey sauce

Tillamook 2 year aged white Cheddar cheese

Toasted brioche bun

TWISTED CORK BISTRO

OMAHA, NE

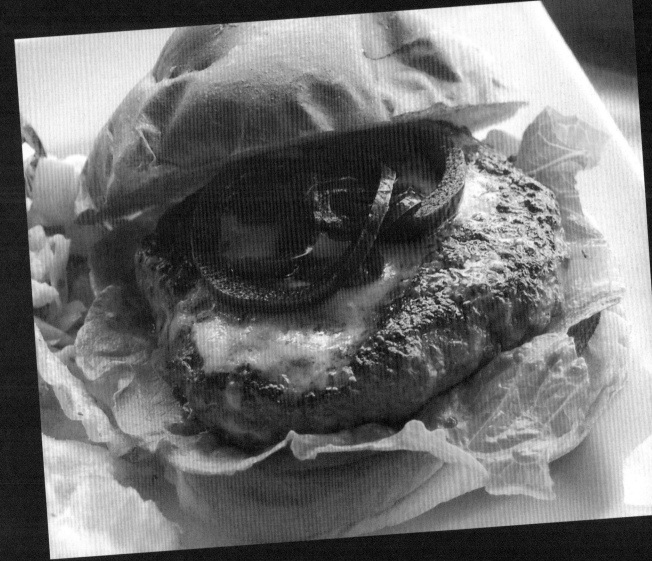

10730 Pacific St. #110, Omaha, NE 68114
(402) 932-1300 • www.twistedcorkbistro.com

What's in it?

Vincent Burger: 4 ounces ground beef, 1 ounce braised short ribs and 1 ounce smoked Gouda

Special Burger Sauce: Tabasco®, mayo, ketchup and cornichons (pickled gherkins)

- *lettuce*
- *tomato*
- *onion*
- *egg bun*

Vincent
A RESTAURANT

1100 NICOLLET MALL, MINNEAPOLIS, MN 55403

(612) 630-1189 • www.vincentarestaurant.com

1710 S. West St., Wichita, KS 67213
(316) 941-3550

What's in it?

2 beef patties	cheese
ketchup	lettuce
mustard	tomato
pickle	toasted bun

Multiple locations
www.bandanasbbq.com

- **St. Louis style ribs**
(hand rubbed and slow smoked to
perfection over hickory logs)

served with two pieces of garlic bread,
Bar-B-Q beans and coleslaw

Multiple Locations
www.birddogbbq.com

WHAT'S IN IT?

chopped oak-smoked, choice-grade brisket combined with slices of spicy hot links

on the side: potato salad and coleslaw

 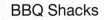

BLACK'S
BARBECUE

Family Owned Since 1932

215 N. Main St., Lockhart, TX 78644
(512) 398-2712, www.blacksbbq.com

What's in it?

- Giant beef ribs (over 1 pound per rib!)
- Pork spare ribs
- Homemade beef and pork sausage
- Certified Angus beef brisket
- Smoked chicken

All pit-smoked to perfection
over post oak wood

THE BRICK PIT

5456 OLD SHELL RD., MOBILE, AL 36608
(251) 343-0001, WWW.BRICKPIT.COM

THE
BRICK
PIT

IT'S
SERIOUS
BAR-B-QUE!

DINE IN OR TAKE OUT
343-0001

WHAT'S IN IT?

- SMOKED BBQ RIBS
- "BRICK PIT" BAR-B-QUE SAUCE
- INCLUDES COLESLAW, BBQ BEANS AND TEXAS TOAST

WHAT'S IN IT?

slow smoked pulled pork shoulder
coleslaw
mild BBQ sauce

2249 Central Ave.

Memphis, TN 38104

901-272-9377

4375 Summer Ave.

Memphis, TN 38122

901-767-4672

www.cbqmemphis.com

CITY MARKET

633 DAVIS ST. ★ LULING, TX 78648
(830) 875-9019

WHAT'S IN IT?

★ BEEF BRISKET, BARBECUED FOR 8 HOURS
★ HOMEMADE SWEET MUSTARD SAUCE
★ RAW ONION SLICES

Clay's Smokehouse

BAD TO THE BONE
PORTLAND, OREGON
~S~

"The ribs here are fall-off-the-bone good, with a tangy sweet sauce that, mercifully, is available in take-home mason jars.

-Portland Monthly
May 2005

CLAY'S SMOKEHOUSE GRILL

2932 SE. Division St., Portland, OR 97202
(503) 235-4755, www.clayssmokehouse.ypguides.net

What's in it?
pork spareribs
Smoked until tender, then braised in our BBQ sauce

**Served with home fries
with garlic sauce,
poppy seed slaw
and Texas
toast**

FIORELLA'S JACK STACK BARBECUE

Multiple locations • www.jackstackbbq.com

WHAT'S IN IT?

- **WELL-MARBLED BEEF SHORT RIBS, SMOKED TO PERFECTION**

Served with your choice of salad and one of the following side items:
hickory pit beans • cheesy corn bake • old-fashioned potato salad
creamy coleslaw • French fries • seasonal vegetables • cheese potato bake
vegetable kabob • baked potato

GERMANTOWN
COMMISSARY

EPICUREAN BBQ & RIBS

2290 Germantown Rd., Germantown, TN 38138
(901) 754-5540, www.commissarybbq.com

What's in it?
- pulled pork
- coleslaw
- BBQ sauce

WORLD'S BEST BBQ
STEAKS ~ SEAFOOD ~ RIBS

HITCHING POST
PRODUCTS

BBQ₂YOU

3325 Point Sal Rd.
Casmalia, CA 93429
(805) 937-6151
(866) 879-4088
www.hitchingpost1.com

WHAT'S IN IT?

- **baby back pork ribs cooked "Santa Maria Style"**
  (barbecued over a live fire of California red oak wood, basted and seasoned with our Hitching Post products during the BBQ process)

The Ostini family has been serving great steaks, ribs and seafood since 1952 at their Casmalia restaurant.

What's in it?

★ beef brisket- prepared with a salt and pepper rub and slow cooked in 50-year-old horizontal brick and steel pits using post oak wood

206 W. 2ND ST.
TAYLOR, TX 76574
(512) 352-6206

WWW.LOUIEMUELLERBARBECUE.COM

576 Haight St., San Francisco, CA 94117
(415) 864-7675
www.memphisminnies.com

"It may well be the finest barbecue
restaurant in the state."

Lolis Eric Elie, *Gourmet Magazine*
June 2002

What's in it?

- Texas-style beef brisket, rubbed with our own special beef rub and slow smoked over white oak for 16 hours

On the side:

- Minnie's Macaroni and Cheese, rich and creamy with extra-sharp Cheddar cheese

- Pit-Smoked Beans, pinto beans combined with house-made sauce and chock-full of smoked meat

- Tart 'n Tangy Slaw, shredded cabbage and vegetables in a nonfat, nondairy dressing

- Potato Salad, seasoned with mustard, sweet relish and hard-boiled eggs

- House-made regional barbecue sauce

913 E. Washington Blvd.
Cuba, MO 65453
(573) 885-6791
www.missourihick.com

What's in it?

- **Half slab of wild cherry-smoked, St. Louis-style spareribs**
- **Homemade baked beans**

- **Cucumbers and onions (Mom's special recipe!)**

All of our meats are seasoned with our special rub and then smoked overnight for 12 full hours. After resting (you would need a rest too if you had just spent the night in a smokehouse!), the meats are ready to serve with your choice of house sauces.

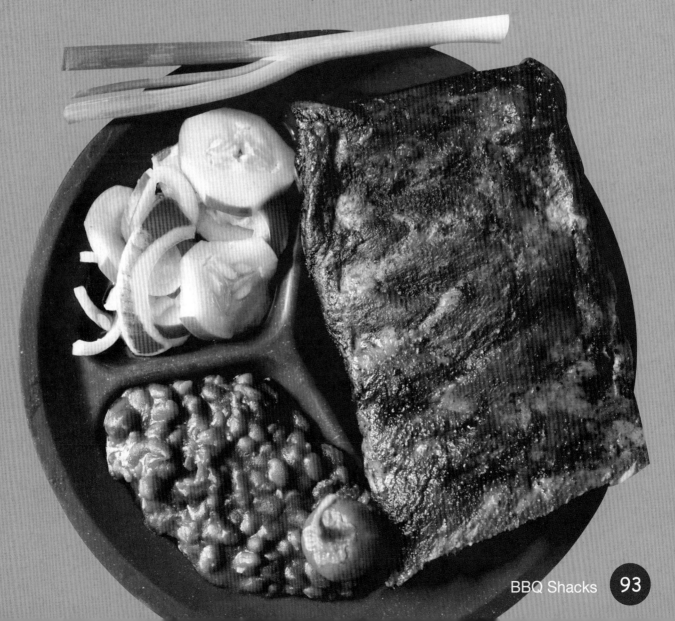

Phil's B·B·Q
San Diego

3750 Sports Arena Blvd. ★ San Diego, CA 92110
(619) 226-6333 ★ www.philsbbq.net

WHAT'S IN IT?

★ Baby back ribs, dry rubbed with a special spice blend, slow cooked over low heat, dipped in Phil's B•B•Q Sauce and finished on a hot mesquite grill

on the side:

★ Colossal hand-dipped golden fried onion rings with house-made buttermilk ranch dressing

328 W. Davie St.

Raleigh, NC 27601

(919) 890-4500

www.thepit-raleigh.com

What's in it?

- ribs (smoked with hickory or oak)
- Eastern North Carolina-style vinegar sauce
- on the side: sweet potato fries and coleslaw

ROPER'S RIBS

BEST BBQ IN THE UNIVERSE

6929 W. Florissant Ave.
St. Louis, MO 63136
(314) 381-6200
www.ropersribs.com

What's in it?

- best-quality beef brisket, rubbed with a special blend of spices and slow smoked 12 hours over green hickory wood

on the side:
- rich and tangy BBQ sauce
- creamy coleslaw

THE SALT LICK
BAR-B-QUE...LIKE NO OTHER!

18300 FM 1826
Driftwood, TX 78619
512-858-4959
www.saltlickbbq.com

What's in it?

- high-quality beef brisket, slow smoked for 16 hours and basted with Original Bar-B-Que Sauce

- delicious Hill Country sausage, the perfect balance of smoke and spice

- tender and tasty pork ribs

Sam's BAR·B·QUE

1110 S. Bascom Ave.

San Jose, CA 95128

(408) 297-9151

www.samsbbq.com

extra-meaty baby back ribs (marinated for 24 hours, then smoked for hours over oak wood)

BBQ SAUCE

THE SHED
BARBEQUE & BLUES JOINT™
A FamilyFoodDrinkery™

Multiple Locations
www.theshedbbq.com

What's in it?

- **spare ribs seasoned with Shed rib rub**
- **Poppa's ShedSpred BBQ Sauce**

on the side: MommaMia's Mac Salad and Daddy O's Creamy Coleslaw

3800 N. Pulaski Rd.
Chicago, IL 60641
773.545.RIBS (7427)
www.smoquebbq.com

WHAT'S IN IT?

St. Louis ribs
(covered with a Memphis-style dry rub to form a savory crust and smoked over apple and oak)

semi-sweet BBQ sauce

516 Main St.
Lexington, TX 78947
(979) 773-4640 (Sat. Only)
(979) 542-8189
www.snowsbbq.com

Snow's BBQ

Best BBQ in Texas

WHAT'S IN IT?

BBQ Brisket
(trimmed brisket that has been slow cooked
for 8 to 10 hours until very tender)

What's in it?

- Texas-style barbecue pork ribs
- melt-in-your-mouth beef brisket
- world famous barbecue sauce
- savory sausage

on the side

- slow cooked BBQ beans
- crowd-pleasing potato salad

What's in it?

- moist and flavorful beef brisket
- tangy barbecue sauce
- homemade bun

on the side

- handmade Texas onion rings

What's in it?

hand-pulled smoked
pork shoulder

BBQ sauce
coleslaw

What's in it?

grilled hot links	onion
cheese	green chiles
chopped beef	BBQ sauce

525 S. Beckham Ave., Tyler, TX 75702
(903) 593-0311
www.stanleyspitbbq.com

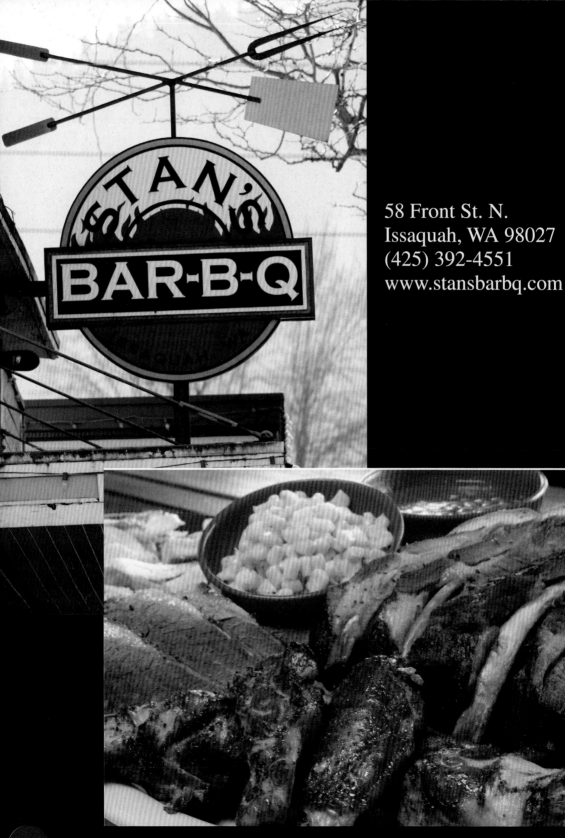

58 Front St. N.
Issaquah, WA 98027
(425) 392-4551
www.stansbarbq.com

WHAT'S IN IT?

3 ribs
$\frac{1}{2}$ pound beef brisket
$\frac{1}{2}$ pound pork
Ceasar salad
baked beans
corn

Multiple Locations
www.supersmokers.com

WHAT'S IN IT?

- Pulled Pork Sandwich (marinated and rotisserie smoked for 15 hours)

- Pulled Chicken Sandwich (marinated and rotisserie smoked for 4 hours)

Pork Loin

Beef Brisket

Turkey

Pork Loin Back Ribs

Half Chicken

Pulled Pork

UBON'S

801 N. Jerry Clower Blvd.
Yazoo City, MS 39194
(662) 716-7100
www.ubons.net

WHAT'S IN IT?

- Pulled pork sandwich (Boston butt rubbed with Ubon's dry rub seasoning and slow smoked with hickory)

on the side:
- Ubon's Bar-B-Que Sauce
- battered hand-cut sweet potato fries

**132 S. CASS AVE., WESTMONT, IL 60559
(630) 493-9000, WWW.UNCLEBUBS.COM**

WHAT'S IN IT?

- highest-quality premium grade pork back ribs
- rubbed with our signature rib seasoning
- slow smoked until tender

on the side:
baked potato and corn bread

What's in it?
- hot links
- ribs
- turkey

on the side:
- homemade coleslaw
- vanized potato served with garlic butter
- Texas Toast

MULTIPLE LOCATIONS THROUGHOUT OKLAHOMA
www.pigstands.com

152 W. 44th St.
New York, NY 10036
212.921.9494
www.virgilsbbq.com

WHAT'S IN IT?

- pulled Carolina pork
- mustard slaw
- sesame seed bun

WHOLE HOG CAFE®

WORLD CHAMPION BBQ

Multiple Locations
www.wholehogcafe.com

WHAT'S IN IT?

- Full slab of award-winning baby back ribs, right off the smoker

- Whole Hog's six signature barbecue sauces

on the side:
- creamy twice-baked potato salad
- hot and hearty baked beans
- cool and tangy coleslaw
- warm home-style dinner roll

79 N. Long Beach Rd.
Rockville Centre, NY 11570

516-678-3878
www.bigelows-rvc.com

delicious!

What's in it?

- Clams dipped in egg wash and milk then deep fried
- Homemade mayo, cocktail sauce, tartar sauce and seasonings
- Relish
- Homemade bun with a corn flour base

bistro 222

22266 Michigan Ave., Dearborn, MI 48124
www.bistro222.com

What's in it?

grilled chicken breast
honey dijon mustard
lettuce
tomato

BORINQUEN
Restaurant

1720 N. California Ave. #1, Chicago, IL 60647, (773) 227-6038 (main location)
3020 N. Central Ave., Chicago, IL 60634, (773) 622-8570
3811 N. Western Ave., Chicago, IL 60618, (773) 442-8001

What's in it?

plantains
American cheese
steak
grilled onions
tomato

romaine lettuce
mayonnaise
minced garlic
dash of seasoning

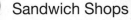

WHAT'S IN IT?

CORNED BEEF
TONGUE
PASTRAMI
SWISS CHEESE
RYE BREAD

What's in it?

- homemade turkey
- cranberry sauce
- stuffing
- mayo
- kaiser roll

Multiple locations:

Arizona

California

Delaware

Florida

Iowa

Maryland

New Jersey

Pennsylvania

Utah

Nevada

Wisconsin

www.capriottis.com

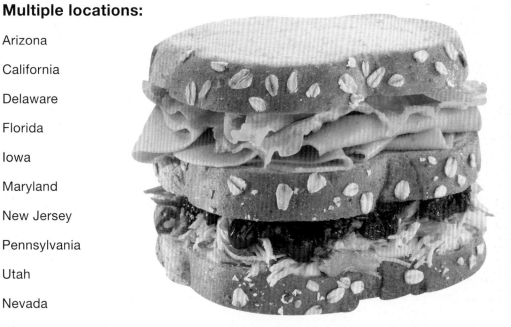

5042 N. CENTRAL AVE.
PHOENIX, AZ 85012
602-266-3636
WWW.CHEESENSTUFFDELI.COM

WHAT'S IN IT?

- BOAR'S HEAD® TURKEY BREAST
- MUENSTER CHEESE
- TOMATO
- PEPPERONCINI
- SHREDDED LETTUCE
- AVOCADO SPREAD
- HOT MUSTARD
- 10-INCH HOAGIE OR SUB ROLL

2605 Wilson Blvd., Arlington, VA 22201
(703) 248-0150
www.earlsinarlington.com

WHAT'S IN IT?
-roasted center-cut pork loin
-fire-roasted red peppers
-bread and butter pickle chips
-chopped yellow onion
-chipotle mayonnaise
-hand-cut deep-fried potatoes
-toasted ciabatta

EAST SIDE POCKETS

FALAFEL ◆ KABOBS ◆ SOUPS ◆ SALADS

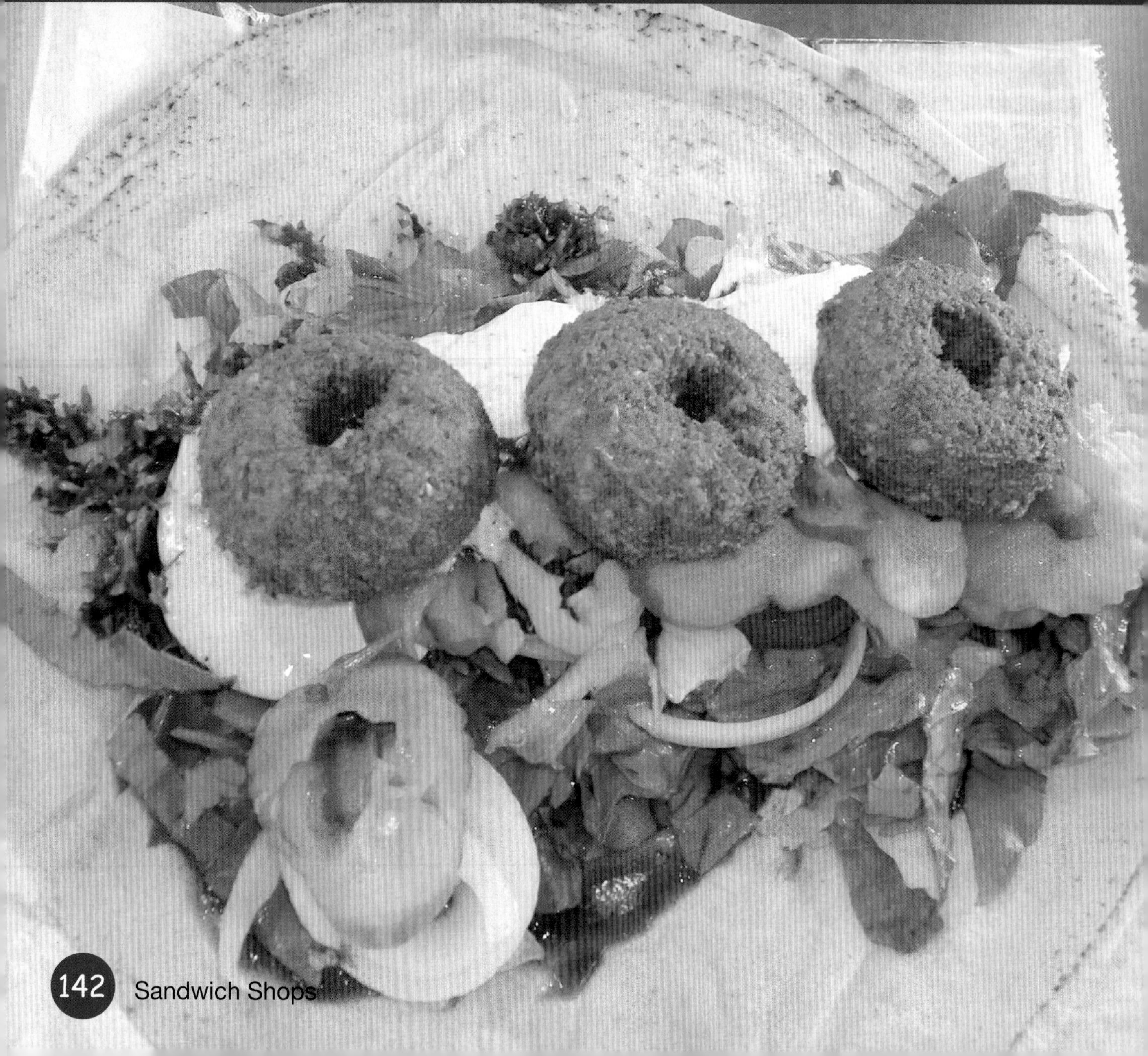

WHAT'S IN IT?

◆ falafel ◆ Syrian bread

topped with your choice of any or all the Toppings:
Hot sauce, Hummus, Lettuce, Tomatoes, Onions, Pickles, Hot Peppers, Tabbouleh, Tahina
(sesame paste, lemon juice, garlic) and Tzaziki (yougert cucumber sauce)

278 Thayer St., Providence, RI 02906
(401) 453-1100
www.eastsidepocket.com

Sandwich Shops 143

What's in it?

- Prosciutto
- Arugula
- Crescenza (soft, mild Cheese)
- Mushrooms
- Spinach
- Goat Cheese

Emporio Rulli

CAFFÈ · PASTICCERIA · WINE BAR

MULTIPLE LOCATIONS · WWW.RULLI.COM

MULTIPLE LOCATIONS
WWW.HI-RISEBREAD.COM

WHAT'S IN IT?

BRINED AND ROASTED TURKEY
MONTEREY JACK CHEESE
AVOCADOS
RUSSIAN DRESSING
SEMOLINA BREAD

WHAT'S IN IT?

- honey ham
- seasoned deli pork
- genoa salami
- Swiss cheese
- mayo
- dill pickles
- mustard
- iceburg lettuce
- tomatoes
- Cuban bread

931 S. Howard Ave., Tampa, FL 33629
(813) 251-2842

3123 Lee Hwy.
Arlington, VA 22201
(703) 528-6266
www.italianstore.com

What's in it?

- homemade dressing
- lettuce
- sweet peppers
- hot peppers
- onions
- Prosciuttini ham
- provolone cheese
- Capacola ham
- Genoa salami
- oregano
- 8-inch Italian crusty sub roll

What's in it?

2 potato pancakes
2 slices Swiss cheese
Thousand Island dressing

kraut
6 ounces thinly sliced
hot corned beef

2855 28th St.
Boulder, CO 80301
303-447-DELI (3354)
www.jimmyanddrews.net

What's in it?

2 slices Swiss cheese
Russian dressing
crispy French fries
3 ounces thinly sliced

hot corned beef
3 ounces thinly sliced
hot pastrami
2 slices rye bread

KATZ'S DELICATESSEN

205 E. Houston St.
New York, NY 10002
(212) 254-2246
www.katzdeli.com

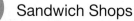

What's in it?
corned beef
sauerkraut
Swiss cheese
Russian dressing
rye bread

Langer's

DELICATESSEN-RESTAURANT

704 S. Alvarado St.
Los Angeles, CA 90057
(213) 483-8050
www.langersdeli.com

What's in it?

- ℒ pastrami
- ℒ coleslaw
- ℒ Swiss cheese
- ℒ Russian dressing
- ℒ seeded rye bread

La Sandwicherie

Miami Beach

229 14th St.
Miami Beach, FL 33139
(305) 532-8934
www.lasandwicherie.com

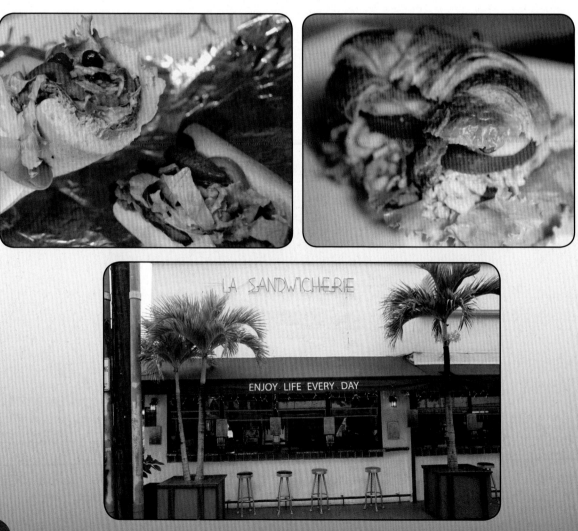

What's in it?

- turkey
- roast beef
- lettuce
- tomatoes
- green and hot peppers
- black olives
- onions
- cucumbers
- cornichons (French pickles)
- mayonnaise
- vinaigrette (French dressing)

Meat Cheese Bread

1406 SE. STARK ST., PORTLAND, OR 97214
503-234-1700 WWW.MEATCHEESEBREAD.COM

What's in it?
egg salad
bacon
lettuce
sweet onion
housemade croissant

"A perfect little taste of Portland...This charming, hole-in-the-wall sandwich-shop-cum-art-gallery combines several local obsessions: unpretentious, everyday fare in the form of carefully crafted sandwiches and salads; local, high-grade ingredients; a friendly, low-key vibe that invites lingering, should you be lucky enough to snag a table." — Doug Perry, *The Oregonian,* June 2009

14718 Detroit Ave.
Lakewood, OH 44107
(216) 226-3699

13463 Cedar Rd.
Cleveland Heights, OH 44118
(216) 965-0988

www.meltbarandgrilled.com

what's in it?

- 2 potato and cheese pierogi
- fresh Napa vodka kraut
- grilled onions
- sharp Cheddar
- 2 (1-inch-thick) slices hearty fresh-baked bread

What's in it?
- green apple
- bacon
- blue cheese

What's in it?
- mushrooms
- cheese
- green peppers
- steak

What's in it?
- ham
- white Cheddar cheese

110 S. 4th Ave. • Franklin, TN 37064
(615) 790-3755 • www.merridees.com

PERRY'S DELI
SINCE 1982
ROAST BEEF • CORNED BEEF • TURKEY • BRISKET • PASTRAMI • HAM

HUNGRY?

Perry's

174 N. Franklin St.
Chicago, IL 60606
(312) 372-7557
www.perrysdeli.com

What's in it?

- thinly sliced lean tender corned beef
- juicy rare roast beef
- coleslaw
- sliced tomato
- Muenster cheese
- homemade Russian dressing

www.pinestatebiscuits.com

3640 SE. Belmont St.
Portland, OR 97214
(503) 236-3346

2204 NE. Alberta St.
Portland, OR 97211
(503) 477-6605

What's in it?

fried chicken   mustard

pickles   honey

WHAT'S IN IT?

• Fresh lobster tossed to order with celery, mayonnaise, lemon juice, salt and pepper

• Served on a buttered, toasted New England-style bun and topped with two pieces of claw meat

on the side:
• Crisp, golden hand-cut Idaho russet French fries

WHAT'S IN IT?

fresh lobster meat (claw and knuckle)

Havarti cheese

fresh herb blend
(thyme, tarragon and chervil)

vine-ripe tomato

sourdough bread

RESTAURANT
BRICCO
SEASONAL ITALIAN

78 Lasalle Rd.
West Hartford, CT 06107
(860) 233-0220
www.billygrant.com

What's in it?

ham	mortadella	mayonnaise
roast beef	American cheese	mustard
prosciutto	provolone cheese	oil & vinegar
pepperoni	lettuce	salt
turkey	tomatoes	pepper
pastrami	onions	oregano
salami	hot & sweet peppers	

HOMEMADE SANDWICHES

SANDWHICH

ON HANDMADE BREAD

407 W. Franklin St.
Chapel Hill, NC 27516
919.929.2114
www.sandwhich.biz

WHAT'S IN IT?

lemon vinaigrette

arugula

tomatoes

marinated sardines

red onion

pickled red chiles

French baguette

Schwabl's

Since 1837

789 Center Rd., West Seneca, NY 14224
(716) 674-9821
www.schwabls.com

What's in it?

roast beef
kümmelweck roll

on the side: coleslaw or pickled beets
and your choice of potato

1145 E. Las Tunas Dr.
San Gabriel, CA 91776
(626) 285-9161
www.stuffedsandwich.com

What's in it?

Your choice of: salami cotto, pepperoni, hard salami, capocollo, mortadella with mozzarella cheese, mustard, mayo, lettuce, tomato and our homemade Italian dressing

- foot-long French roll

What's in it?

- thinly sliced pastrami
- regular or spicy mustard
- dipped in our special homemade broth
- foot-long French roll

1305 E. Franklin St.,
Chapel Hill, NC 27514
(919) 933-1324

What's in it?

- deep-fried breaded buttermilk chicken breast fillet
- freshly baked biscuit

may add on: Cheddar cheese, egg, lettuce, tomato or grilled onions

TOWN HALL
DELICATESSEN

Birthplace of the Sloppy Joe

60 Valley St., South Orange, NJ 07079, (973) 762-4900, www.townhalldeli.com

WHAT'S IN IT?

Russian dressing
coleslaw
roast beef
turkey
Swiss cheese
rye or Russian rye bread

The
Vermont
Country
Deli

436 Western Ave.
Brattleboro, VT 05301
(802) 257-9254

HIGHWAY HAM

ROAD FOOD 6.99 plus tax

VERMONT VEGGIE

I-91 ITALIAN

CRANBERRY SAUCE
MAYONNAISE
CHEDDAR CHEESE
and TURKEY

HORSERADISH SAUCE, DELI MUSTARD, ROAST BEEF and CHEDDAR CHEESE

RUSSIAN DRESSING
SWISS CHEESE
TURKEY
SLICED PICKLES
SPROUTS and LETTUCE

ALL OF THE ABOVE SERVED WITH LETTUCE. and ONION

WHAT'S IN IT?

cranberry sauce

mayonnaise

Cheddar cheese

turkey

lettuce

tomato

red onion

soft wheat roll

What's in it?

Zingerman's corned beef
Switzerland Swiss cheese
sauerkraut
Russian dressing
Jewish rye bread

422 Detroit St.
Ann Arbor, MI 48104
(734) 663-3354
www.zingermansdeli.com

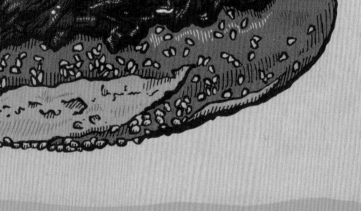

"Oooh, that's good.
Lord have mercy."

–Oprah Winfrey
on #97 Lisa C's Boisterous Brisket

Burger Joints

Becks Prime Restaurants
Multiple Locations
www.becksprime.com

Big Jud's
1289 Protest Rd., Boise, ID 83706
(208) 343-4439
www.bigjudsboise.com

Black Iron Burger Shop
540 E. 5th St., New York, NY 10009
(212) 677-6067
www.blackironburger.com

Burger Station
113 E. 7th Ave., Winfield, KS 67156
(620) 221-9773

Butcher & Singer
1500 Walnut St., Philadelphia, PA 19102
(215) 732-4444
www.butcherandsinger.com

The Counter
Multiple Locations
www.thecounterburger.com

The Cozy Inn Hamburgers
108 N. 7th St., Salina, KS 67401
(785) 825-2699
www.cozyburger.com

The Cutting Board
307 Dewey Ave., Eureka, MT 59917
(406) 297-6090
www.thecuttingboard.biz

Denny's Beer Barrel Pub
1452 Woodland Rd., Clearfield, PA 16830
(814) 765-7190
www.dennysbeerbarrelpub.com

Hemmer Brothers
230 S. Phillips Ave., #101, Sioux Falls, SD 57104
(605) 334-3301

Hi Boy
Multiple Locations
www.hiboydrivein.com

Huey's
Multiple Locations
www.hueyburger.com

Kuma's Corner
2900 W. Belmont Ave., Chicago, IL 60618
(773) 604-8769
www.kumascorner.com

Lunchbox Laboratory
7302 15th Ave. NW., Seattle, WA 98117
(206) 706-3092
www.lunchboxlaboratory.com

Miner Dunn
8940 Indianapolis Blvd., Highland, IN 46322
(219) 923-3311

Murphy's
11 S. Main St., Hanover, NH 03755
(603) 643-4075
www.murphysonthegreen.com

Pearl's Deluxe Burgers
708 Post St., San Francisco, CA 94109
(415) 409-6120
www.pearlsburgers.com

Poag Mahone's
333 S. Wells St., Chicago, IL 60604
(312) 566-9100
www.poagmahones.com

Radius
8 High St., Boston, MA 02110
(617) 426-1234
www.radiusrestaurant.com

Rosebud Restaurants
Multiple Locations
www.rosebudrestaurants.com

Rouge
205 S. 18th St., Philadelphia, PA 19103
(215) 732-6622
www.rouge98.com

Slap Daddy's
914 Baytree Rd., Valdosta, GA 31602
(229) 244-1966
www.slapdaddys.com

Slow Bar
533 SE. Grand Ave., Portland, OR 97214
(503) 230-7767
www.slowbar.net

Sobelmans Pub-N-Grill
1900 W. St. Paul Ave., Milwaukee, WI 53233
(414) 931-1919
www.milwaukeesbestburgers.com

Solly's Grille
4629 N. Port Washington Rd., Glendale, WI 53212
(414) 332-8808

Sugar Shack
22495 Hwy. 385, Deadwood, SD 57732
(605) 341-6772

Teddy's Bigger Burgers
Multiple Locations
www.teddysbiggerburgers.com

The Thurman Cafe
183 Thurman Ave., Columbus, OH 43206
(614) 443-1570
www.thethurmancafe.com

25 degrees
Multiple Locations
www.25degreesrestaurant.com

Twisted Cork Bistro
10730 Pacific St., #110, Omaha, NE 68114
(402) 932-1300
www.twistedcorkbistro.com

Vincent - A Restaurant
1100 Nicollet Mall, Minneapolis, MN 55403
(612) 630-1189
www.vincentarestaurant.com

Walt's Famous Hamburgers
1710 S. West St., Wichita, KS 67213
(316) 941-3550

BBQ Shacks

Bandana's Bar-B-Q
Multiple Locations
www.bandanasbbq.com

Bird Dog BBQ
Multiple Locations
www.birddogbbq.com

Black's Barbecue
215 N. Main St., Lockhart, TX 78644
(512) 398-2712
www.blacksbbq.com

The Brick Pit
5456 Old Shell Rd., Mobile, AL 36608
(251) 343-0001
www.brickpit.com

Central BBQ
Multiple Locations
www.cbqmemphis.com

City Market
633 Davis St., Luling, TX 78648
(830) 875-9019

Clay's Smokehouse Grill
2932 SE. Division St., Portland, OR 97202
(503) 235-4755
www.clayssmokehouse.ypguides.net

Fiorella's Jack Stack Barbecue
Multiple Locations
www.jackstackbbq.com

Germantown Commissary
2290 Germantown Rd., Germantown, TN 38138
(901) 754-5540
www.commissarybbq.com

The Hitching Post
3325 Point Sal Rd., Casmalia, CA 93429
(805) 937-6151, (866) 879-4088
www.hitchingpost1.com

Louie Mueller Barbecue
206 W. 2nd St., Taylor, TX 76574
(512) 352-6206
www.louiemuellerbarbecue.com

Memphis Minnie's
576 Haight St., San Francisco, CA 94117
(415) 864-7675
www.memphisminnies.com

Missouri Hick BBQ
913 E. Washington Blvd., Cuba, MO 65453
(573) 885-6791
www.missourihick.com

Phil's BBQ
3750 Sports Arena Blvd., San Diego, CA 92110
(619) 226-6333
www.philsbbq.net

The Pit Authentic Barbecue
328 W. Davie St., Raleigh, NC 27601
(919) 890-4500
www.thepit-raleigh.com

Roper's Ribs
6929 W. Florissant Ave., St. Louis, MO 63136
(314) 381-6200
www.ropersribs.com

The Salt Lick Bar-B-Que
18300 FM 1826, Driftwood, TX 78619
(512) 858-4959
www.saltlickbbq.com

Sam's Bar•B•Que
1110 S. Bascom Ave., San Jose, CA 95128
(408) 297-9151
www.samsbbq.com

The Shed Barbeque & Blues Joint
Multiple Locations
www.theshedbbq.com

Smoque BBQ
3800 N. Pulaski Rd., Chicago, IL 60641
(773) 545-7427
www.smoquebbq.com

Snow's BBQ
516 Main St., Lexington, TX 78947
(979) 773-4640 (Sat. only)
www.snowsbbq.com

Sonny Bryan's Smokehouse
Multiple Locations
www.sonnybryans.com

Stanley's Famous Pit Bar-B-Q
525 S. Beckham Ave., Tyler, TX 75702
(903) 593-0311
www.stanleyspitbbq.com

Stan's Bar-B-Q
58 Front St. N., Issaquah, WA 98027
(425) 392-4551
www.stansbarbq.com

Super Smokers BBQ
Multiple Locations
www.supersmokers.com

Ubon's Restaurant
801 N. Jerry Clower Blvd., Yazoo City, MS 39194
(662) 716-7100
www.ubons.net

Uncle's Bub's
132 S. Cass Ave., Westmont, IL 60559
(630) 493-9000
www.unclebubs.com

Van's Pig Stands
Multiple Locations
www.pigstands.com

Virgil's Real Barbecue
152 W. 44th St., New York, NY 10036
(212) 921-9494
www.virgilsbbq.com

Whole Hog Café
Multiple Locations
www.wholehogcafe.com

Sandwich Shops

Bigelow's
79 N. Long Beach Rd., Rockville Centre, NY 11570
(516) 678-3878
www.bigelows-rvc.com

Bistro 222
22266 Michigan Ave., Dearborn, MI 48124
(313) 792-7500
www.bistro222.com

Borinquen Restaurant
Multiple Locations
(773) 227-6038 (main location)

Canter's Delicatessen
Multiple Locations
www.cantersdeli.com

Capriotti's Sandwich Shop
Multiple Locations
www.capriottis.com

Cheese 'n Stuff
5042 N. Central Ave., Phoenix, AZ 85012
602-266-3636
www.cheesenstuffdeli.com

Earl's Sandwiches
2605 Wilson Blvd., Arlington, VA 22201
(703) 248-0150
www.earlsinarlington.com

East Side Pockets
278 Thayer St., Providence, RI 02906
(401) 453-1100
www.eastsidepocket.com

Emporio Rulli
Multiple Locations
www.rulli.com

Hi-Rise Bread Company
Multiple Locations
www.hi-risebread.com

Hugo's Spanish Restaurant
931 S. Howard Ave., Tampa, FL 33629
(813) 251-2842

The Italian Store
3123 Lee Hwy., Arlington, VA 22201
(703) 528-6266
www.italianstore.com

Jimmy & Drew's 28th Street Deli
2855 28th St., Boulder, CO 80301
(303) 447-3354
www.jimmyanddrews.net

Katz's Delicatessen
205 E. Houston St., New York, NY 10002
(212) 254-2246
www.katzdeli.com

Langer's Delicatessen-Restaurant
704 S. Alvarado St., Los Angeles, CA 90057
(213) 483-8050
www.langersdeli.com

La Sandwicherie
229 14th St., Miami Beach, FL 33139
(305) 532-8934
www.lasandwicherie.com

Meat Cheese Bread
1406 SE. Stark St., Portland, OR 97214
503-234-1700
www.meatcheesebread.com

Melt Bar and Grilled
Multiple Locations
www.meltbarandgrilled.com

Merridee's Breadbasket
110 S. 4th Ave., Franklin, TN 37064
(615) 790-3755
www.merridees.com

Perry's Deli
174 N. Franklin St., Chicago, IL 60606
(312) 372-7557
www.perrysdeli.com

Pine State Biscuits
Multiple Locations
www.pinestatebiscuits.com

The Rod Barn
47 Old Post Rd., Ghent, NY 12075
(518) 828-6677
www.redbarnfood.com

Restaurant Bricco
78 Lasalle Rd., West Hartford, CT 06107
(860) 233-0220
www.billygrant.com

Sal, Kris, & Charlie's Deli
33-12 23rd Ave., Astoria, NY 11102
(718) 278-9240

Sandwhich
407 W. Franklin St., Chapel Hill, NC 27516
(919) 929-2114
www.sandwhich.biz

Schwabl's Restaurant
789 Center Rd., West Seneca, NY 14224
(716) 674-9821
www.schwabls.com

The Stuffed Sandwich
1145 E. Las Tunas Dr., San Gabriel, CA 91776
(626) 285-9161
www.stuffedsandwich.com

Sunrise Biscuit Kitchen
1305 E. Franklin St., Chapel Hill, NC 27514
(919) 933-1324

Town Hall Delicatessen
60 Valley St., South Orange, NJ 07079
(973) 762-4900
www.townhalldeli.com

The Vermont Country Deli
436 Western Ave., Brattleboro, VT 05301
(802) 257-9254

Zingerman's Deli
422 Detroit St., Ann Arbor, MI 48104
(734) 663-3354
www.zingermansdeli.com